Inspiration & Gratitude
Guided Daily Journal
202 Pages with Daily Prompts
Two Page Spread per Day

_____

_____

_____

"Feeling gratitude and not expressing it is like wrapping a present and not giving it."

- William Arthur Ward

Today's Reflections

Date: _____ Day: _____ Mood: _____

Intention for the day / week / month / year: _____

Today I am truly grateful for:

_____

_____

_____

My feelings today:

_____

_____

_____

Today's Essentials:

_____

_____

_____

_____

Anything bothering me?

_____

_____

_____

If only...

_____

_____

_____

Today in seven words or less:

_____

_____

Today's Reflections

Date: _____ Day: _____ Mood: _____

Intention for the day / week / month / year: _____

Today I am truly grateful for:

_____

_____

_____

My feelings today:

_____

_____

_____

Today's Essentials:

_____

_____

_____

_____

Anything bothering me?

_____

_____

_____

If only...

_____

_____

_____

Today in seven words or less:

_____

_____

Today's Reflections

Date: _____ *Day:* _____ *Mood:* _____

Intention for the day / week / month / year: _____

Today I am truly grateful for:

_____

_____

_____

My feelings today:

_____

_____

_____

Today's Essentials:

_____

_____

_____

_____

Anything bothering me?

_____

_____

_____

If only...

_____

_____

_____

Today in seven words or less:

_____

_____

Today's Reflections

Date: _____ Day: _____ Mood: _____

Intention for the day / week / month / year: _____

Today I am truly grateful for:

_____

_____

_____

My feelings today:

_____

_____

_____

Today's Essentials:

_____

_____

_____

_____

Anything bothering me?

_____

_____

_____

If only...

_____

_____

_____

Today in seven words or less:

_____

_____

Today's Reflections

Date: _____ Day: _____ Mood: _____

Intention for the day / week / month / year: _____

Today I am truly grateful for:

_____

_____

_____

My feelings today:

_____

_____

_____

Today's Essentials:

_____

_____

_____

_____

Anything bothering me?

_____

_____

_____

If only...

_____

_____

_____

Today in seven words or less:

_____

_____

Today's Reflections

Date: _____ Day: _____ Mood: _____

Intention for the day / week / month / year: _____

Today I am truly grateful for:

_____

_____

_____

My feelings today:

_____

_____

_____

Today's Essentials:

_____

_____

_____

_____

Anything bothering me?

_____

_____

_____

If only...

_____

_____

_____

Today in seven words or less:

_____

_____

Today's Reflections

Date: _____ Day: _____ Mood: _____

Intention for the day / week / month / year: _____

Today I am truly grateful for:

_____

_____

_____

My feelings today:

_____

_____

_____

Today's Essentials:

_____

_____

_____

_____

Anything bothering me?

_____

_____

_____

If only...

_____

_____

_____

Today in seven words or less:

_____

_____

Today's Reflections

Date: _____ Day: _____ Mood: _____

Intention for the day / week / month / year: _____

Today I am truly grateful for:

_____

_____

_____

My feelings today:

_____

_____

_____

Today's Essentials:

_____

_____

_____

_____

Anything bothering me?

_____

_____

_____

If only...

_____

_____

_____

Today in seven words or less:

_____

_____

Today's Reflections

Date: _____ *Day:* _____ *Mood:* _____

Intention for the day / week / month / year: _____

Today I am truly grateful for:

_____

_____

_____

My feelings today:

_____

_____

_____

Today's Essentials:

_____

_____

_____

_____

Anything bothering me?

_____

_____

_____

If only...

_____

_____

_____

Today in seven words or less:

_____

_____

Today's Reflections

Date: _____ Day: _____ Mood: _____

Intention for the day / week / month / year: _____

Today I am truly grateful for:

_____

_____

_____

My feelings today:

_____

_____

_____

Today's Essentials:

_____

_____

_____

_____

Anything bothering me?

_____

_____

_____

If only...

_____

_____

_____

Today in seven words or less:

_____

_____

Today's Reflections

Date: _____ Day: _____ Mood: _____

Intention for the day / week / month / year: _____

Today I am truly grateful for:

_____

_____

_____

My feelings today:

_____

_____

_____

Today's Essentials:

_____

_____

_____

_____

Anything bothering me?

_____

_____

_____

If only...

_____

_____

_____

Today in seven words or less:

_____

_____

Today's Reflections

Date: _____ *Day:* _____ *Mood:* _____

Intention for the day / week / month / year: _____

Today I am truly grateful for:

_____

_____

_____

My feelings today:

_____

_____

_____

Today's Essentials:

_____

_____

_____

_____

Anything bothering me?

_____

_____

_____

If only...

_____

_____

_____

Today in seven words or less:

_____

_____

Today's Reflections

Date: _____ Day: _____ Mood: _____

Intention for the day / week / month / year: _____

Today I am truly grateful for:

_____

_____

_____

My feelings today:

_____

_____

_____

Today's Essentials:

_____

_____

_____

_____

Anything bothering me?

_____

_____

_____

If only...

_____

_____

_____

Today in seven words or less:

_____

_____

Today's Reflections

Date: _____ Day: _____ Mood: _____

Intention for the day / week / month / year: _____

Today I am truly grateful for:

_____

_____

_____

My feelings today:

_____

_____

_____

Today's Essentials:

_____

_____

_____

_____

Anything bothering me?

_____

_____

_____

If only...

_____

_____

_____

Today in seven words or less:

_____

_____

Today's Reflections

Date: _____ Day: _____ Mood: _____

Intention for the day / week / month / year: _____

Today I am truly grateful for:

_____

_____

_____

My feelings today:

_____

_____

_____

Today's Essentials:

_____

_____

_____

_____

Anything bothering me?

_____

_____

_____

If only...

_____

_____

_____

Today in seven words or less:

_____

_____

Today's Reflections

Date: _____ Day: _____ Mood: _____

Intention for the day / week / month / year: _____

Today I am truly grateful for:

_____

_____

_____

My feelings today:

_____

_____

_____

Today's Essentials:

_____

_____

_____

_____

Anything bothering me?

_____

_____

_____

If only...

_____

_____

_____

Today in seven words or less:

_____

_____

Today's Reflections

Date: _____ Day: _____ Mood: _____

Intention for the day / week / month / year: _____

Today I am truly grateful for:

_____

_____

_____

My feelings today:

_____

_____

_____

Today's Essentials:

_____

_____

_____

_____

Anything bothering me?

_____

_____

_____

If only...

_____

_____

_____

Today in seven words or less:

_____

_____

Today's Reflections

Date: _____ *Day:* _____ *Mood:* _____

Intention for the day / week / month / year: _____

Today I am truly grateful for:

_____

_____

_____

My feelings today:

_____

_____

_____

Today's Essentials:

_____

_____

_____

_____

Anything bothering me?

_____

_____

_____

If only...

_____

_____

_____

Today in seven words or less:

_____

_____

Today's Reflections

Date: _____ *Day:* _____ *Mood:* _____

Intention for the day / week / month / year: _____

Today I am truly grateful for:

_____

_____

_____

My feelings today:

_____

_____

_____

Today's Essentials:

_____

_____

_____

_____

Anything bothering me?

_____

_____

_____

If only...

_____

_____

_____

Today in seven words or less:

_____

_____

Today's Reflections

Date: _____ Day: _____ Mood: _____

Intention for the day / week / month / year: _____

Today I am truly grateful for:

_____

_____

_____

My feelings today:

_____

_____

_____

Today's Essentials:

_____

_____

_____

_____

Anything bothering me?

_____

_____

_____

If only...

_____

_____

_____

Today in seven words or less:

_____

_____

Today's Reflections

Date: _____ Day: _____ Mood: _____

Intention for the day / week / month / year: _____

Today I am truly grateful for:

_____

_____

_____

My feelings today:

_____

_____

_____

Today's Essentials:

_____

_____

_____

_____

Anything bothering me?

_____

_____

_____

If only...

_____

_____

_____

Today in seven words or less:

_____

_____

Today's Reflections

Date: _____   Day: _____   Mood: _____

Intention for the day / week / month / year: _____

Today I am truly grateful for:

_____

_____

_____

My feelings today:

_____

_____

_____

Today's Essentials:

_____

_____

_____

_____

Anything bothering me?

_____

_____

_____

If only...

_____

_____

_____

Today in seven words or less:

_____

_____

Today's Reflections

Date: _____ Day: _____ Mood: _____

Intention for the day / week / month / year: _____

Today I am truly grateful for:

_____

_____

_____

My feelings today:

_____

_____

_____

Today's Essentials:

_____

_____

_____

_____

Anything bothering me?

_____

_____

_____

If only...

_____

_____

_____

Today in seven words or less:

_____

_____

Today's Reflections

Date: _____ *Day:* _____ *Mood:* _____

Intention for the day / week / month / year: _____

Today I am truly grateful for:

_____

_____

_____

My feelings today:

_____

_____

_____

Today's Essentials:

_____

_____

_____

_____

Anything bothering me?

_____

_____

_____

If only...

_____

_____

_____

Today in seven words or less:

_____

_____

Today's Reflections

Date: _____ Day: _____ Mood: _____

Intention for the day / week / month / year: _____

Today I am truly grateful for:

_____

_____

_____

My feelings today:

_____

_____

_____

Today's Essentials:

_____

_____

_____

_____

Anything bothering me?

_____

_____

_____

If only...

_____

_____

_____

Today in seven words or less:

_____

_____

Today's Reflections

Date: _____   Day: _____   Mood: _____

Intention for the day / week / month / year: _____

Today I am truly grateful for:

_____

_____

_____

My feelings today:

_____

_____

_____

Today's Essentials:

_____

_____

_____

_____

Anything bothering me?

_____

_____

_____

If only...

_____

_____

_____

Today in seven words or less:

_____

_____

Today's Reflections

Date: _____ Day: _____ Mood: _____

Intention for the day / week / month / year: _____

Today I am truly grateful for:

_____

_____

_____

My feelings today:

_____

_____

_____

Today's Essentials:

_____

_____

_____

_____

Anything bothering me?

_____

_____

_____

If only...

_____

_____

_____

Today in seven words or less:

_____

_____

Today's Reflections

Date: _____ *Day:* _____ *Mood:* _____

Intention for the day / week / month / year: _____

Today I am truly grateful for:

_____

_____

_____

My feelings today:

_____

_____

_____

Today's Essentials:

_____

_____

_____

_____

Anything bothering me?

_____

_____

_____

If only...

_____

_____

_____

Today in seven words or less:

_____

_____

Today's Reflections

Date: _____ Day: _____ Mood: _____

Intention for the day / week / month / year: _____

Today I am truly grateful for:

_____

_____

_____

My feelings today:

_____

_____

_____

Today's Essentials:

_____

_____

_____

_____

Anything bothering me?

_____

_____

If only...

_____

_____

_____

Today in seven words or less:

_____

_____

Today's Reflections

Date: _____   Day: _____   Mood: _____

Intention for the day / week / month / year: _____

Today I am truly grateful for:

_____

_____

_____

My feelings today:

_____

_____

_____

Today's Essentials:

_____

_____

_____

_____

Anything bothering me?

_____

_____

_____

If only...

_____

_____

_____

Today in seven words or less:

_____

_____

Today's Reflections

Date: _____ Day: _____ Mood: _____

Intention for the day / week / month / year: _____

Today I am truly grateful for:

_____

_____

_____

My feelings today:

_____

_____

_____

Today's Essentials:

_____

_____

_____

_____

Anything bothering me?

_____

_____

_____

If only...

_____

_____

_____

Today in seven words or less:

_____

_____

Today's Reflections

Date: _____ Day: _____ Mood: _____

Intention for the day / week / month / year: _____

Today I am truly grateful for:

_____

_____

_____

My feelings today:

_____

_____

_____

Today's Essentials:

_____

_____

_____

_____

Anything bothering me?

_____

_____

_____

If only...

_____

_____

_____

Today in seven words or less:

_____

_____

Today's Reflections

Date: _____ Day: _____ Mood: _____

Intention for the day / week / month / year: _____

Today I am truly grateful for:

_____

_____

_____

My feelings today:

_____

_____

_____

Today's Essentials:

_____

_____

_____

_____

Anything bothering me?

_____

_____

_____

If only...

_____

_____

_____

Today in seven words or less:

_____

_____

Today's Reflections

Date: _____ Day: _____ Mood: _____

Intention for the day / week / month / year: _____

Today I am truly grateful for:

_____

_____

_____

My feelings today:

_____

_____

_____

Today's Essentials:

_____

_____

_____

_____

Anything bothering me?

_____

_____

_____

If only...

_____

_____

_____

Today in seven words or less:

_____

_____

Today's Reflections

Date: _____   Day: _____   Mood: _____

Intention for the day / week / month / year: _____

Today I am truly grateful for:

_____

_____

_____

My feelings today:

_____

_____

_____

Today's Essentials:

_____

_____

_____

_____

Anything bothering me?

_____

_____

_____

If only...

_____

_____

_____

Today in seven words or less:

_____

_____

Today's Reflections

Date: _____ Day: _____ Mood: _____

Intention for the day / week / month / year: _____

Today I am truly grateful for:

_____

_____

_____

My feelings today:

_____

_____

_____

Today's Essentials:

_____

_____

_____

_____

Anything bothering me?

_____

_____

If only...

_____

_____

_____

Today in seven words or less:

_____

_____

Today's Reflections

Date: _____ *Day:* _____ *Mood:* _____

Intention for the day / week / month / year: _____

Today I am truly grateful for:

_____

_____

_____

My feelings today:

_____

_____

_____

Today's Essentials:

_____

_____

_____

_____

Anything bothering me?

_____

_____

_____

If only...

_____

_____

_____

Today in seven words or less:

_____

_____

Today's Reflections

Date: _____ Day: _____ Mood: _____

Intention for the day / week / month / year: _____

Today I am truly grateful for:

_____

_____

_____

My feelings today:

_____

_____

_____

Today's Essentials:

_____

_____

_____

_____

Anything bothering me?

_____

_____

_____

If only...

_____

_____

_____

Today in seven words or less:

_____

_____

Today's Reflections

Date: _____ Day: _____ Mood: _____

Intention for the day / week / month / year: _____

Today I am truly grateful for:

_____

_____

_____

My feelings today:

_____

_____

_____

Today's Essentials:

_____

_____

_____

_____

Anything bothering me?

_____

_____

_____

If only...

_____

_____

_____

Today in seven words or less:

_____

_____

Today's Reflections

Date: _____   Day: _____   Mood: _____

Intention for the day / week / month / year: _____

Today I am truly grateful for:

_____

_____

_____

My feelings today:

_____

_____

_____

Today's Essentials:

_____

_____

_____

_____

Anything bothering me?

_____

_____

_____

If only...

_____

_____

_____

Today in seven words or less:

_____

_____

Today's Reflections

Date: _____ Day: _____ Mood: _____

Intention for the day / week / month / year: _____

Today I am truly grateful for:

_____

_____

_____

My feelings today:

_____

_____

_____

Today's Essentials:

_____

_____

_____

_____

Anything bothering me?

_____

_____

If only...

_____

_____

_____

Today in seven words or less:

_____

_____

Today's Reflections

Date: _____ Day: _____ Mood: _____

Intention for the day / week / month / year: _____

Today I am truly grateful for:

_____

_____

_____

My feelings today:

_____

_____

_____

Today's Essentials:

_____

_____

_____

_____

Anything bothering me?

_____

_____

_____

If only...

_____

_____

_____

Today in seven words or less:

_____

_____

Today's Reflections

Date: _____   Day: _____   Mood: _____

Intention for the day / week / month / year: _____

Today I am truly grateful for:

_____

_____

_____

My feelings today:

_____

_____

_____

Today's Essentials:

_____

_____

_____

_____

Anything bothering me?

_____

_____

_____

If only...

_____

_____

_____

Today in seven words or less:

_____

_____

Today's Reflections

Date: _____ Day: _____ Mood: _____

Intention for the day / week / month / year: _____

Today I am truly grateful for:

_____

_____

_____

My feelings today:

_____

_____

_____

Today's Essentials:

_____

_____

_____

_____

Anything bothering me?

_____

_____

_____

If only...

_____

_____

_____

Today in seven words or less:

_____

_____

Today's Reflections

Date: _____   Day: _____   Mood: _____

Intention for the day / week / month / year: _____

Today I am truly grateful for:

_____

_____

_____

My feelings today:

_____

_____

_____

Today's Essentials:

_____

_____

_____

_____

Anything bothering me?

_____

_____

_____

If only...

_____

_____

_____

Today in seven words or less:

_____

_____

Today's Reflections

Date: _____ *Day:* _____ *Mood:* _____

Intention for the day / week / month / year: _____

Today I am truly grateful for:

_____

_____

_____

My feelings today:

_____

_____

_____

Today's Essentials:

_____

_____

_____

_____

Anything bothering me?

_____

_____

_____

If only...

_____

_____

_____

Today in seven words or less:

_____

_____

Today's Reflections

Date: _____ Day: _____ Mood: _____

Intention for the day / week / month / year: _____

Today I am truly grateful for:

_____

_____

_____

My feelings today:

_____

_____

_____

Today's Essentials:

_____

_____

_____

_____

Anything bothering me?

_____

_____

_____

If only...

_____

_____

_____

Today in seven words or less:

_____

_____

Today's Reflections

Date: _____   Day: _____   Mood: _____

Intention for the day / week / month / year: _____

Today I am truly grateful for:

_____

_____

_____

My feelings today:

_____

_____

_____

Today's Essentials:

_____

_____

_____

_____

Anything bothering me?

_____

_____

_____

If only...

_____

_____

_____

Today in seven words or less:

_____

_____

Today's Reflections

Date: _____ Day: _____ Mood: _____

Intention for the day / week / month / year: _____

Today I am truly grateful for:

_____

_____

_____

My feelings today:

_____

_____

_____

Today's Essentials:

_____

_____

_____

_____

Anything bothering me?

_____

_____

_____

If only...

_____

_____

_____

Today in seven words or less:

_____

_____

Today's Reflections

Date: _____ Day: _____ Mood: _____

Intention for the day / week / month / year: _____

Today I am truly grateful for:

_____

_____

_____

My feelings today:

_____

_____

_____

Today's Essentials:

_____

_____

_____

_____

Anything bothering me?

_____

_____

_____

If only...

_____

_____

_____

Today in seven words or less:

_____

_____

Today's Reflections

Date: _____ Day: _____ Mood: _____

Intention for the day / week / month / year: _____

Today I am truly grateful for:

_____

_____

_____

My feelings today:

_____

_____

_____

Today's Essentials:

_____

_____

_____

_____

Anything bothering me?

_____

_____

_____

If only...

_____

_____

_____

Today in seven words or less:

_____

_____

Today's Reflections

Date: _____   Day: _____   Mood: _____

Intention for the day / week / month / year: _____

Today I am truly grateful for:

_____

_____

_____

My feelings today:

_____

_____

_____

Today's Essentials:

_____

_____

_____

_____

Anything bothering me?

_____

_____

_____

If only...

_____

_____

_____

Today in seven words or less:

_____

_____

Today's Reflections

Date: _____ *Day:* _____ *Mood:* _____

Intention for the day / week / month / year: _____

Today I am truly grateful for:

_____

_____

_____

My feelings today:

_____

_____

_____

Today's Essentials:

_____

_____

_____

_____

Anything bothering me?

_____

_____

_____

If only...

_____

_____

_____

Today in seven words or less:

_____

_____

Today's Reflections

Date: _____ Day: _____ Mood: _____

Intention for the day / week / month / year: _____

Today I am truly grateful for:

_____

_____

_____

My feelings today:

_____

_____

_____

Today's Essentials:

_____

_____

_____

_____

Anything bothering me?

_____

_____

_____

If only...

_____

_____

_____

Today in seven words or less:

_____

_____

Today's Reflections

Date: _____ Day: _____ Mood: _____

Intention for the day / week / month / year: _____

Today I am truly grateful for:

_____

_____

_____

My feelings today:

_____

_____

_____

Today's Essentials:

_____

_____

_____

_____

Anything bothering me?

_____

_____

_____

If only...

_____

_____

_____

Today in seven words or less:

_____

_____

Today's Reflections

Date: _____ Day: _____ Mood: _____

Intention for the day / week / month / year: _____

Today I am truly grateful for:

_____

_____

_____

My feelings today:

_____

_____

_____

Today's Essentials:

_____

_____

_____

_____

Anything bothering me?

_____

_____

_____

If only...

_____

_____

_____

Today in seven words or less:

_____

_____

Today's Reflections

Date: _____ Day: _____ Mood: _____

Intention for the day / week / month / year: _____

Today I am truly grateful for:

_____

_____

_____

My feelings today:

_____

_____

_____

Today's Essentials:

_____

_____

_____

_____

Anything bothering me?

_____

_____

_____

If only...

_____

_____

_____

Today in seven words or less:

_____

_____

Today's Reflections

Date: _____ *Day:* _____ *Mood:* _____

Intention for the day / week / month / year: _____

Today I am truly grateful for:

_____

_____

_____

My feelings today:

_____

_____

_____

Today's Essentials:

_____

_____

_____

_____

Anything bothering me?

_____

_____

_____

If only...

_____

_____

_____

Today in seven words or less:

_____

_____

Today's Reflections

Date: _____ *Day:* _____ *Mood:* _____

Intention for the day / week / month / year: _____

Today I am truly grateful for:

_____

_____

_____

My feelings today:

_____

_____

_____

Today's Essentials:

_____

_____

_____

_____

Anything bothering me?

_____

_____

_____

If only...

_____

_____

_____

Today in seven words or less:

_____

_____

Today's Reflections

Date: _____ Day: _____ Mood: _____

Intention for the day / week / month / year: _____

Today I am truly grateful for:

_____

_____

_____

My feelings today:

_____

_____

_____

Today's Essentials:

_____

_____

_____

_____

Anything bothering me?

_____

_____

_____

If only...

_____

_____

_____

Today in seven words or less:

_____

_____

Today's Reflections

Date: _____ Day: _____ Mood: _____

Intention for the day / week / month / year: _____

Today I am truly grateful for:

_____

_____

_____

My feelings today:

_____

_____

_____

Today's Essentials:

_____

_____

_____

_____

Anything bothering me?

_____

_____

_____

If only...

_____

_____

_____

Today in seven words or less:

_____

_____

Today's Reflections

Date: _____ Day: _____ Mood: _____

Intention for the day / week / month / year: _____

Today I am truly grateful for:

_____

_____

_____

My feelings today:

_____

_____

_____

Today's Essentials:

_____

_____

_____

_____

Anything bothering me?

_____

_____

_____

If only...

_____

_____

_____

Today in seven words or less:

_____

_____

Today's Reflections

Date: _____ *Day:* _____ *Mood:* _____

Intention for the day / week / month / year: _____

Today I am truly grateful for:

_____

_____

_____

My feelings today:

_____

_____

_____

Today's Essentials:

_____

_____

_____

_____

Anything bothering me?

_____

_____

_____

If only...

_____

_____

_____

Today in seven words or less:

_____

_____

Today's Reflections

Date: _____ Day: _____ Mood: _____

Intention for the day / week / month / year: _____

Today I am truly grateful for:

_____

_____

_____

My feelings today:

_____

_____

_____

Today's Essentials:

_____

_____

_____

_____

Anything bothering me?

_____

_____

_____

If only...

_____

_____

_____

Today in seven words or less:

_____

_____

Today's Reflections

Date: _____ Day: _____ Mood: _____

Intention for the day / week / month / year: _____

Today I am truly grateful for:

_____

_____

_____

My feelings today:

_____

_____

_____

Today's Essentials:

_____

_____

_____

_____

Anything bothering me?

_____

_____

_____

If only...

_____

_____

_____

Today in seven words or less:

_____

_____

Today's Reflections

Date: _____ Day: _____ Mood: _____

Intention for the day / week / month / year: _____

Today I am truly grateful for:

_____

_____

_____

My feelings today:

_____

_____

_____

Today's Essentials:

_____

_____

_____

_____

Anything bothering me?

_____

_____

_____

If only...

_____

_____

_____

Today in seven words or less:

_____

_____

Today's Reflections

Date: _____ Day: _____ Mood: _____

Intention for the day / week / month / year: _____

Today I am truly grateful for:

_____

_____

_____

My feelings today:

_____

_____

_____

Today's Essentials:

_____

_____

_____

_____

Anything bothering me?

_____

_____

_____

If only...

_____

_____

_____

Today in seven words or less:

_____

_____

Today's Reflections

Date: _____ Day: _____ Mood: _____

Intention for the day / week / month / year: _____

Today I am truly grateful for:

_____

_____

_____

My feelings today:

_____

_____

_____

Today's Essentials:

_____

_____

_____

_____

Anything bothering me?

_____

_____

_____

If only...

_____

_____

_____

Today in seven words or less:

_____

_____

Today's Reflections

Date: _____   *Day:* _____   *Mood:* _____

Intention for the day / week / month / year: _____

Today I am truly grateful for:

_____

_____

_____

My feelings today:

_____

_____

_____

Today's Essentials:

_____

_____

_____

_____

Anything bothering me?

_____

_____

_____

If only...

_____

_____

_____

Today in seven words or less:

_____

_____

Today's Reflections

Date: _____ Day: _____ Mood: _____

Intention for the day / week / month / year: _____

Today I am truly grateful for:

_____

_____

_____

My feelings today:

_____

_____

_____

Today's Essentials:

_____

_____

_____

_____

Anything bothering me?

_____

_____

_____

If only...

_____

_____

_____

Today in seven words or less:

_____

_____

Today's Reflections

Date: _____ Day: _____ Mood: _____

Intention for the day / week / month / year: _____

Today I am truly grateful for:

_____

_____

_____

My feelings today:

_____

_____

_____

Today's Essentials:

_____

_____

_____

_____

Anything bothering me?

_____

_____

_____

If only...

_____

_____

_____

Today in seven words or less:

_____

_____

Today's Reflections

Date: _____ Day: _____ Mood: _____

Intention for the day / week / month / year: _____

Today I am truly grateful for:

_____

_____

_____

My feelings today:

_____

_____

_____

Today's Essentials:

_____

_____

_____

_____

Anything bothering me?

_____

_____

_____

If only...

_____

_____

_____

Today in seven words or less:

_____

_____

Today's Reflections

Date: _____ *Day:* _____ *Mood:* _____

Intention for the day / week / month / year: _____

Today I am truly grateful for:

_____

_____

_____

My feelings today:

_____

_____

_____

Today's Essentials:

_____

_____

_____

_____

Anything bothering me?

_____

_____

_____

If only...

_____

_____

_____

Today in seven words or less:

_____

_____

Today's Reflections

Date: _____ *Day:* _____ *Mood:* _____

Intention for the day / week / month / year: _____

Today I am truly grateful for:

_____

_____

_____

My feelings today:

_____

_____

_____

Today's Essentials:

_____

_____

_____

_____

Anything bothering me?

_____

_____

_____

If only...

_____

_____

_____

Today in seven words or less:

_____

_____

Today's Reflections

Date: _____ Day: _____ Mood: _____

Intention for the day / week / month / year: _____

Today I am truly grateful for:

_____

_____

_____

My feelings today:

_____

_____

_____

Today's Essentials:

_____

_____

_____

_____

Anything bothering me?

_____

_____

_____

If only...

_____

_____

_____

Today in seven words or less:

_____

_____

Today's Reflections

Date: _____ Day: _____ Mood: _____

Intention for the day / week / month / year: _____

Today I am truly grateful for:

_____

_____

_____

My feelings today:

_____

_____

_____

Today's Essentials:

_____

_____

_____

_____

Anything bothering me?

_____

_____

_____

If only...

_____

_____

_____

Today in seven words or less:

_____

_____

Today's Reflections

Date: _____ *Day:* _____ *Mood:* _____

Intention for the day / week / month / year: _____

Today I am truly grateful for:

_____

_____

_____

My feelings today:

_____

_____

_____

Today's Essentials:

_____

_____

_____

_____

Anything bothering me?

_____

_____

_____

If only...

_____

_____

_____

Today in seven words or less:

_____

_____

Today's Reflections

Date: _____ Day: _____ Mood: _____

Intention for the day / week / month / year: _____

Today I am truly grateful for:

_____

_____

_____

My feelings today:

_____

_____

_____

Today's Essentials:

_____

_____

_____

_____

Anything bothering me?

_____

_____

_____

If only...

_____

_____

_____

Today in seven words or less:

_____

_____

Today's Reflections

Date: _____ Day: _____ Mood: _____

Intention for the day / week / month / year: _____

Today I am truly grateful for:

_____

_____

_____

My feelings today:

_____

_____

_____

Today's Essentials:

_____

_____

_____

_____

Anything bothering me?

_____

_____

_____

If only...

_____

_____

_____

Today in seven words or less:

_____

_____

Today's Reflections

Date: _____ *Day:* _____ *Mood:* _____

Intention for the day / week / month / year: _____

Today I am truly grateful for:

_____

_____

_____

My feelings today:

_____

_____

_____

Today's Essentials:

_____

_____

_____

_____

Anything bothering me?

_____

_____

_____

If only...

_____

_____

_____

Today in seven words or less:

_____

_____

Today's Reflections

Date: _____   Day: _____   Mood: _____

Intention for the day / week / month / year: _____

Today I am truly grateful for:

_____

_____

_____

My feelings today:

_____

_____

_____

Today's Essentials:

_____

_____

_____

_____

Anything bothering me?

_____

_____

_____

If only...

_____

_____

_____

Today in seven words or less:

_____

_____

Today's Reflections

Date: _____ Day: _____ Mood: _____

Intention for the day / week / month / year: _____

Today I am truly grateful for:

_____

_____

_____

My feelings today:

_____

_____

_____

Today's Essentials:

_____

_____

_____

_____

Anything bothering me?

_____

_____

_____

If only...

_____

_____

_____

Today in seven words or less:

_____

_____

Today's Reflections

Date: _____ *Day:* _____ *Mood:* _____

Intention for the day / week / month / year: _____

Today I am truly grateful for:

_____

_____

_____

My feelings today:

_____

_____

_____

Today's Essentials:

_____

_____

_____

_____

Anything bothering me?

_____

_____

_____

If only...

_____

_____

_____

Today in seven words or less:

_____

_____

Today's Reflections

Date: _____ Day: _____ Mood: _____

Intention for the day / week / month / year: _____

Today I am truly grateful for:

_____

_____

_____

My feelings today:

_____

_____

_____

Today's Essentials:

_____

_____

_____

_____

Anything bothering me?

_____

_____

_____

If only...

_____

_____

_____

Today in seven words or less:

_____

_____

Today's Reflections

Date: _____ Day: _____ Mood: _____

Intention for the day / week / month / year: _____

Today I am truly grateful for:

_____

_____

_____

My feelings today:

_____

_____

_____

Today's Essentials:

_____

_____

_____

_____

Anything bothering me?

_____

_____

_____

If only...

_____

_____

_____

Today in seven words or less:

_____

_____

Today's Reflections

Date: _____ Day: _____ Mood: _____

Intention for the day / week / month / year: _____

Today I am truly grateful for:

_____

_____

_____

My feelings today:

_____

_____

_____

Today's Essentials:

_____

_____

_____

_____

Anything bothering me?

_____

_____

_____

If only...

_____

_____

_____

Today in seven words or less:

_____

_____

Today's Reflections

Date: _____ Day: _____ Mood: _____

Intention for the day / week / month / year: _____

Today I am truly grateful for:

_____

_____

_____

My feelings today:

_____

_____

_____

Today's Essentials:

_____

_____

_____

_____

Anything bothering me?

_____

_____

_____

If only...

_____

_____

_____

Today in seven words or less:

_____

_____

Today's Reflections

Date: _____ Day: _____ Mood: _____

Intention for the day / week / month / year: _____

Today I am truly grateful for:

_____

_____

_____

My feelings today:

_____

_____

_____

Today's Essentials:

_____

_____

_____

_____

Anything bothering me?

_____

_____

_____

If only...

_____

_____

_____

Today in seven words or less:

_____

_____

Today's Reflections

Date: _____ Day: _____ Mood: _____

Intention for the day / week / month / year: _____

Today I am truly grateful for:

_____

_____

_____

My feelings today:

_____

_____

_____

Today's Essentials:

_____

_____

_____

_____

Anything bothering me?

_____

_____

_____

If only...

_____

_____

_____

Today in seven words or less:

_____

_____

Today's Reflections

Date: _____ *Day:* _____ *Mood:* _____

Intention for the day / week / month / year: _____

Today I am truly grateful for:

_____

_____

_____

My feelings today:

_____

_____

_____

Today's Essentials:

_____

_____

_____

_____

Anything bothering me?

_____

_____

_____

If only...

_____

_____

_____

Today in seven words or less:

_____

_____

Today's Reflections

Date: _____ Day: _____ Mood: _____

Intention for the day / week / month / year: _____

Today I am truly grateful for:

_____

_____

_____

My feelings today:

_____

_____

_____

Today's Essentials:

_____

_____

_____

_____

Anything bothering me?

_____

_____

_____

If only...

_____

_____

_____

Today in seven words or less:

_____

_____

Today's Reflections

Date: _____ Day: _____ Mood: _____

Intention for the day / week / month / year: _____

Today I am truly grateful for:

_____

_____

_____

My feelings today:

_____

_____

_____

Today's Essentials:

_____

_____

_____

_____

Anything bothering me?

_____

_____

_____

If only...

_____

_____

_____

Today in seven words or less:

_____

_____

Today's Reflections

Date: _____ Day: _____ Mood: _____

Intention for the day / week / month / year: _____

Today I am truly grateful for:

_____

_____

_____

My feelings today:

_____

_____

_____

Today's Essentials:

_____

_____

_____

_____

Anything bothering me?

_____

_____

_____

If only...

_____

_____

_____

Today in seven words or less:

_____

_____

Today's Reflections

Date: _____ Day: _____ Mood: _____

Intention for the day / week / month / year: _____

Today I am truly grateful for:

_____

_____

_____

My feelings today:

_____

_____

_____

Today's Essentials:

_____

_____

_____

_____

Anything bothering me?

_____

_____

_____

If only...

_____

_____

_____

Today in seven words or less:

_____

_____

Today's Reflections

Date: _____ Day: _____ Mood: _____

Intention for the day / week / month / year: _____

Today I am truly grateful for:

_____

_____

_____

My feelings today:

_____

_____

_____

Today's Essentials:

_____

_____

_____

_____

Anything bothering me?

_____

_____

_____

If only...

_____

_____

_____

Today in seven words or less:

_____

_____

Today's Reflections

Date: _____ *Day:* _____ *Mood:* _____

Intention for the day / week / month / year: _____

Today I am truly grateful for:

_____

_____

_____

My feelings today:

_____

_____

_____

Today's Essentials:

_____

_____

_____

_____

Anything bothering me?

_____

_____

_____

If only...

_____

_____

_____

Today in seven words or less:

_____

_____

Today's Reflections

Date: _____   Day: _____   Mood: _____

Intention for the day / week / month / year: _____

Today I am truly grateful for:

_____

_____

_____

My feelings today:

_____

_____

_____

Today's Essentials:

_____

_____

_____

_____

Anything bothering me?

_____

_____

_____

If only...

_____

_____

_____

Today in seven words or less:

_____

_____

Today's Reflections

Date: _____ Day: _____ Mood: _____

Intention for the day / week / month / year: _____

Today I am truly grateful for:

_____

_____

_____

My feelings today:

_____

_____

_____

Today's Essentials:

_____

_____

_____

_____

Anything bothering me?

_____

_____

_____

If only...

_____

_____

_____

Today in seven words or less:

_____

_____

Today's Reflections

Date: _____ Day: _____ Mood: _____

Intention for the day / week / month / year: _____

Today I am truly grateful for:

_____

_____

_____

My feelings today:

_____

_____

_____

Today's Essentials:

_____

_____

_____

_____

Anything bothering me?

_____

_____

_____

If only...

_____

_____

_____

Today in seven words or less:

_____

_____

Today's Reflections

Date: _____   Day: _____   Mood: _____

Intention for the day / week / month / year: _____

Today I am truly grateful for:

_____

_____

_____

My feelings today:

_____

_____

_____

Today's Essentials:

_____

_____

_____

_____

Anything bothering me?

_____

_____

_____

If only...

_____

_____

_____

Today in seven words or less:

_____

_____

Final Reflections